ORIENTEERING

BY ISABEL TEITELBAUM

childsworld.com

Published by The Child's World®
800-599-READ • www.childsworld.com

Photography Credits
Photographs ©: Shutterstock Images, cover, 1, 5, 8, 11; Paya Mona/Shutterstock Images, 6; Igor Stramyk/Shutterstock Images, 7; iStockphoto, 12, 15, 17; 19, 20; Mikhail Pankov/Shutterstock Images, 13, 18

ISBN Information
9781503869806 (Reinforced Library Binding)
9781503881020 (Portable Document Format)
9781503882331 (Online Multi-user eBook)
9781503883642 (Electronic Publication)

LCCN 2022951181

Printed in the United States of America

ABOUT THE AUTHOR

Isabel Teitelbaum has a degree in journalism from the University of Minnesota. She has written about an array of topics from environmental issues to groundbreaking research studies. Growing up on Lake Superior, she fell in love with hiking and outdoor sports.

Contents

CHAPTER ONE

WHAT IS ORIENTEERING?

Olivia runs on the park trail. She has a map in one hand and a compass in the other. Olivia looks down at her map to make sure she's heading in the right direction. She sees her next control point on the map. It is the last one. Control points are checkpoints along an orienteering route. The control point is marked on the map with a purple circle. It looks like the control point will be next to a large tree. The tree is marked on the map with a green circle. Olivia runs faster. The person who finds all the control points the fastest wins the orienteering event. Orienteering is a sport created to test a person's **navigation** skills. Using only a map and compass, people try to find certain spots outdoors.

Olivia reaches a large pine tree. It is the same one that is marked on the map with a green circle. Orienteering maps are different from regular maps. Orienteering maps have different patterns, **symbols**, and colors to show landmarks on each course. These landmarks help Olivia find the control points.

Orienteers must be able to read maps and make quick decisions as they navigate a course.

Many orienteers use compasses with flat bases because they are light and can be set down on a map.

Olivia spots the control point. It is marked with an orange-and-white flag hanging from a tree branch. She checks into the control point with her timing card. Every participant carries one of these cards. They are often called finger sticks. They record which control points orienteers have found and how fast they reach them.

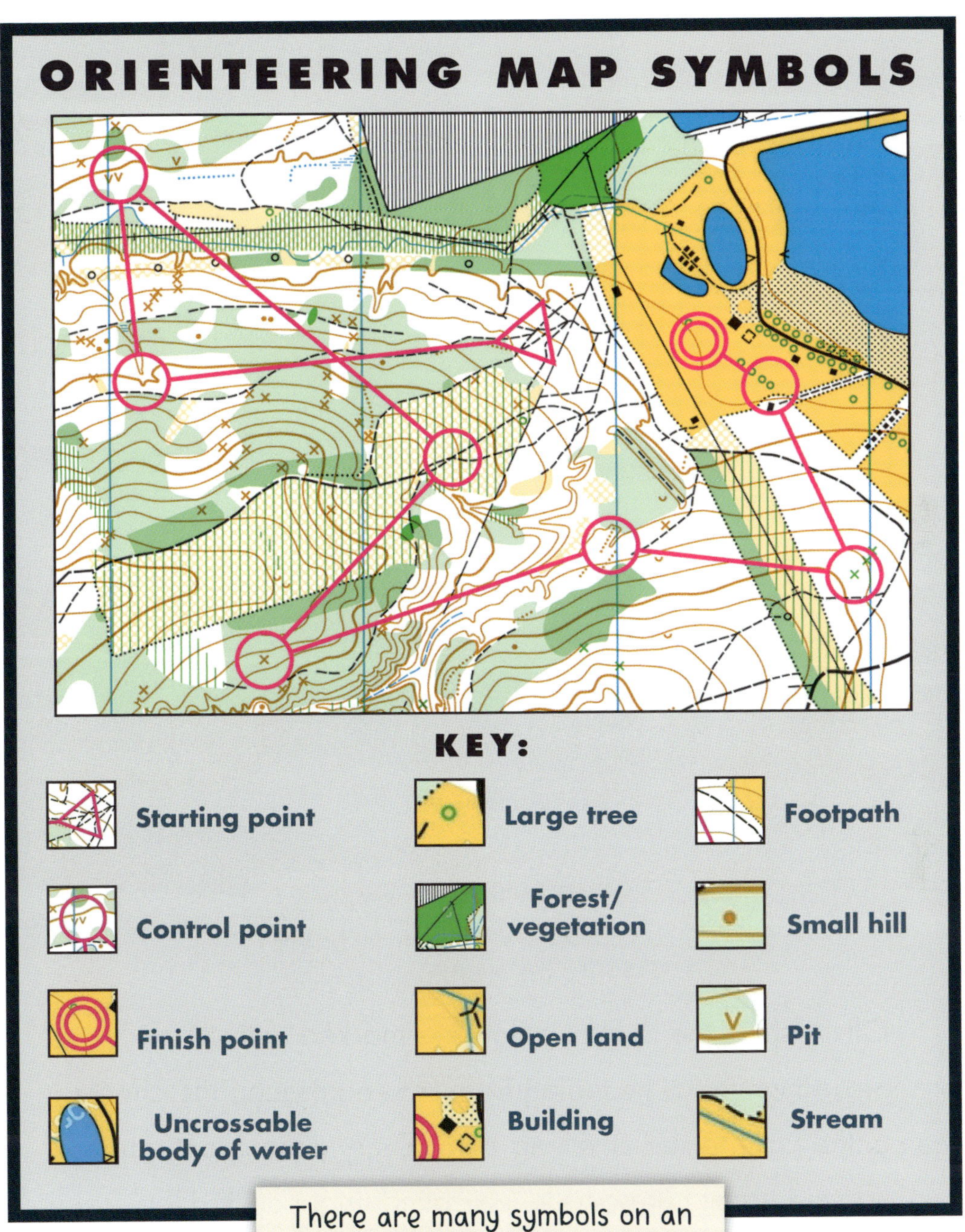

There are many symbols on an orienteering map. The purple lines show the orienteering route.

At control points, orienteers check-in by inserting their finger sticks into an electronic device.

Now that Olivia has reached all the control points, she can rush to the finish point. She gets third place in the event. She is very excited to tell her parents. Her legs are tired, and she is out of breath. But she is already thinking about future orienteering events. Next time she hopes to get first place.

Olivia has been part of the Delaware Valley Orienteering Association for two years. It is the oldest orienteering club in the United States. It was founded in 1967. When Olivia first joined the club, she didn't know how to read a map. But now she uses her map-reading skills to lead camping trips.

Orienteering has been around for a long time. It started in Sweden in 1918 and became popular in Scandinavia. After World War II (1939–1945), orienteering began to spread as a sport around the world. It was also used to improve soldiers' navigation skills so they could find their way through new areas. Today, orienteering is a sport that many people enjoy.

TOPOGRAPHICAL MAPS

Orienteering maps are topographical with extra orienteering landmarks. Topographical maps use lines to show the elevation of areas above or below sea level. This can show people where hills or valleys are. It helps them understand how steep the land is. The maps can also show how deep a body of water is.

CHAPTER TWO

WHO ORIENTEERS?

People orienteer all over the world. The sport became so popular in Europe that the International Orienteering Federation (IOF) was created in 1961. Orienteering was recognized as an Olympic sport in 1977.

Some people orienteer just for fun. It allows them to get outdoors and practice their navigation skills. It's a great way for people to explore nature and practice **self-reliance**. Orienteering can be done in mountains, forests, cities, and parks.

People can orienteer on their own or with a group. People who take the sport more seriously can participate in longer orienteering events as part of a team. This is called rogaining. In rogaining, control points are set up on a course. Teams try to reach as many control points as they can to earn points within a time limit.

There are many orienteering clubs in the United States. These clubs allow people to meet up with other orienteers. They might have a few members or hundreds of members.

Some people participate in orienteering races as a team. Team members must work together to navigate a course.

Not all types of orienteering involve races. Some people like to orienteer at their own pace, experiencing nature with family and friends.

In rogaining, orienteers plan the best route to reach as many control points as possible.

Some people become very good at orienteering. They participate in events across the United States or travel to other countries. People can compete in different kinds of orienteering. The most common kind is traditional orienteering. This involves walking or running to find control points. Some orienteering events involve skiing or mountain biking while searching for control points.

RADIO ORIENTEERING

Radio orienteering, or fox hunting, was used by soldiers in World War II. They used it to practice locating people with their radios. In radio orienteering, the control points are **transmitters**. They send out a signal for people to pick up on their own radios. Some people call these radio orienteering control points "foxes."

People can also participate in trail orienteering. This is not timed like traditional orienteering. Instead, a person is scored on how accurately she can recognize **decoys** and control points from the map. Some people enjoy night orienteering, too. This is when people do orienteering courses in the dark with a headlamp.

As a person gets more comfortable with reading a map, he can try more difficult courses. The courses labeled white on the map are the shortest and easiest. They can take less than 20 minutes to complete. The longest and most difficult courses are marked blue. These can take one to three hours to complete.

In 2016, World Orienteering Day was made a holiday by the IOF. It is celebrated every year on a different day in May. On this day, people introduce others to the sport.

In mountain bike orienteering, people can use map holders that attach to their bikes. This makes it easier to read the map while biking.

Many people enjoy orienteering. They usually have good **sportsmanship** and want others to join the friendly competition. Some people like the sense of accomplishment they feel after completing a course.

CHAPTER THREE

ORIENTEERING RESPONSIBLY

For the best orienteering experience, there are some important things participants need to remember. Orienteering is a very active sport. It's a great way to get exercise. But it also requires preparation. Most people wear athletic clothes and tennis shoes so they can stay comfortable. Wearing long sleeves helps protect people from cuts or scrapes. Some people bring water and snacks, especially for longer courses. When orienteering, all wrappers and bottles taken on the course should be brought home.

People should remember to orienteer responsibly. The sport has a strong focus on respecting the environment. People should make sure they don't leave any litter or equipment behind. When people leave the land just as they found it, they help protect animal habitats. Habitats are places where plants and animals live. People can also help prevent erosion, or the wearing away of the land by water, wind, or human activity. An orienteer can protect the environment by staying on the course marked on her map.

For longer courses, orienteers should come prepared with snacks, water bottles, and comfortable clothes.

Orienteering maps mark which areas of land people should avoid. Responsible orienteers always follow the course on their maps.

Studies in Australia, Denmark, England, and Canada looked at the impacts of orienteering. Orienteering is very popular in these countries. The studies showed that orienteering had a low environmental impact.

There are also websites where people can create their own orienteering maps. They can make maps for areas that do not have courses yet. It can be exciting to explore a new area, but the IOF encourages people to respect the land. It is important for people to make sure they have permission to use the land for orienteering.

In most events, orienteers are required to carry a safety whistle.

People who are new to orienteering should start with easier courses or events held in smaller parks. They should also prepare themselves physically for orienteering. People should not choose courses that are too hard for them. Stretching before orienteering is a great way to warm up and avoid injury. Often, people are orienteering in unfamiliar areas. Trails can be rocky or slippery.

On orienteering courses, some areas are out-of-bounds. All participants must stay within the boundaries listed on their map.

If a person is going orienteering alone, she should first tell someone where she is going. It is also important to bring the necessary supplies. A compass and a map are the two most important things to have. A whistle is helpful, too. If a person gets injured while orienteering, she can use it to call for help. Whistles can also help people find orienteers who get lost.

Orienteering is a very inclusive sport. People of all ages and abilities can participate. String orienteering is sometimes used for kids. It is a safe way for them to try orienteering. They follow a string that leads them on an exciting path. This is usually done in a smaller area than normal orienteering courses.

There are only a few rules to follow during an orienteering event. During races, people should stay as quiet as possible and avoid interfering with other teams. In traditional orienteering, the only pieces of equipment allowed are a map and a compass.

Orienteering is an inexpensive and nature-friendly activity. It allows many people to explore beautiful trails they have never seen before. There are a lot of fun events that people can participate in year-round. Some people orienteer without competing in events. People can orienteer with their families on the weekend or by themselves just for fun. People can learn more about orienteering through local clubs and orienteering events. To get started, check out a local group!

GLOSSARY

decoys (DEE-koyz) Decoys are things meant to confuse people by looking like something else. On orienteering courses, there are decoys that look like control points to try to confuse people.

elevation (eh-luh-VAY-shuhn) Elevation is how much higher a piece of land is than sea level. Orienteering maps use elevation markings and symbols to tell people when they will be going up a hill.

navigation (nah-vuh-GAY-shuhn) Navigation is the process of accurately finding a location by following a route. To improve their navigation skills, people can practice reading a map and using a compass.

self-reliance (SELF-ree-LYE-uhns) To have self-reliance means to rely only on one's own abilities and resources. Orienteers show self-reliance by not relying on GPS to help them find locations.

sportsmanship (SPORTS-muhn-ship) Sportsmanship means having kind and respectful behavior toward others during an event. People can show good sportsmanship by congratulating the winner after an orienteering event.

symbols (SIM-buhls) Symbols are images or signs used to represent something else. On orienteering maps, black square symbols represent buildings.

transmitters (trans-MIH-tuhrs) Transmitters are equipment that send out electrical signals to radios or televisions. People use radios to locate transmitters during radio orienteering events.

FAST FACTS

- Orienteering began in Sweden in 1918. After World War II, it began to spread as a sport around the world.
- Orienteering was a training exercise for soldiers to prepare them for war.
- Orienteering for a longer event as part of a team is called rogaining. Some people compete in events while others choose to orienteer on their own for fun.
- People can orienteer year-round. There is hiking, biking, skiing, and radio orienteering.
- People should remember to follow safety rules and respect the environment when orienteering.

ONE STRIDE FURTHER

- People enjoy orienteering for lots of reasons. What do you think people might learn or gain from participating in the sport?
- Are you interested in trying orienteering? Why or why not? Who is someone you would like to try orienteering with?
- Why do you think it is important to be respectful of the land while orienteering? What are some ways you can practice being kind to the environment while orienteering?

FIND OUT MORE

IN THE LIBRARY

Aschim, Hans. *How to Go Anywhere (and Not Get Lost): A Guide to Navigation for Young Adventurers.* New York, NY: Workman Publishing, 2021.

Maurer, Tracy Nelson. *Using Topographic Maps.* Minneapolis, MN: Lerner Publications, 2017.

Miles, Justin. *Ultimate Mapping Guide for Kids.* Richmond Hill, ON, Canada: Firefly Books, 2016.

ON THE WEB

Visit our website for links about orienteering:
childsworld.com/links

Note to Parents, Caregivers, Teachers, and Librarians: We routinely verify our Web links to make sure they are safe and active sites. So encourage your readers to check them out!

INDEX